This book belongs to

_____

This book is dedicated to my children - Mikey, Kobe, and Jojo.
Sharing is caring.

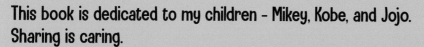

Sharing Ninja

☆

By Mary Nhin

Pictures by
Jelena Stupar

I like stuff. Lots of stuff.

And whatever I had, I used to like to keep to myself.

"Touch my stuff, and you're toast!" I'd say to my sister if she went upstairs.

"Be careful with my stuff, please," I'd say to my mom when she cleaned my room. I even made a sign for my toy closet door which read...Sharing Ninja's stuff! KEEP OUT!!

I was just the same at school. If someone asked to borrow a pencil or a crayon, I'd always say...

In the cafeteria, I'd guard my lunchbox like a dog with a bone.

And if anyone wanted to play with the ball, my answer was always the same...

"You're strange," my best friend, Humble Ninja, would say. We'd been close since kindergarten. Sometimes, Humble Ninja didn't know why we were still friends. But then, I wasn't mean about everything. I was just a bit selfish when it came to my stuff.

One thing we liked doing together was hiking in the woods in my backyard. We'd leave at sunrise with a picnic, and sometimes trek for a couple of hours. When we found the right spot, we'd camp and spend the day messing around. It was a great adventure.

After packing my stuff, I grabbed my backpack
and said goodbye to my mom and dad.

As we headed off on our adventure, it was a beautiful, warm day.

On many of our trips, we followed a tried and trusted path down to a meadow with a small stream alongside. It was the perfect spot for a picnic. We had spent lots of happy times there, lounging about in the sunshine and swimming in the cool, crystal water.

On the new route, we explored for hours and found lizards and insects we never saw before.

After a while, we decided to sit down to have lunch.

As I opened my backpack, I began to pull out things I didn't recognize. Then, I realized I had accidentally picked up the wrong backpack while leaving the house.

Humble Ninja got out a lunch box, picked up two of the four sandwiches inside, and laid them on a plate in front of me.

We began eating. Halfway through a second sandwich, Humble Ninja reached into the backpack for a bag of chips, tearing them open and pouring half onto my napkin.

For the rest of the afternoon, we had a wonderful time - running through the meadow, climbing trees, and playing in a small stream.

That night, as I laid in bed, I thought about my friend's kindness.

The next day, I invited Humble Ninja over to hang out.

Sharing Ninja's Poem

Sharing is great and sharing is kind,
It's one of the best feelings you'll find.

It doesn't take much to go the extra mile,
And it'll make the ones you care for smile.

So, if you see someone who doesn't have much.
Sharing is caring with a magical touch.

Remembering to share could be your
secret weapon against selfishness.

Please visit us at ninjalifehacks.tv to check out our box sets!

@marynhin   @GrowGrit
#NinjaLifeHacks

Mary Nhin   Ninja Life Hacks

Ninja Life Hacks